EXPLORING THE STATES

Washington

THE EVERGREEN STATE

by Kristin Schuetz

BLASTOFF! 5 READERS

BELLWETHER MEDIA • MINNEAPOLIS, MN

Note to Librarians, Teachers, and Parents:

Blastoff! Readers are carefully developed by literacy experts and combine standards-based content with developmentally appropriate text.

Level 1 provides the most support through repetition of high-frequency words, light text, predictable sentence patterns, and strong visual support.

Level 2 offers early readers a bit more challenge through varied simple sentences, increased text load, and less repetition of high-frequency words.

Level 3 advances early-fluent readers toward fluency through increased text and concept load, less reliance on visuals, longer sentences, and more literary language.

Level 4 builds reading stamina by providing more text per page, increased use of punctuation, greater variation in sentence patterns, and increasingly challenging vocabulary.

Level 5 encourages children to move from "learning to read" to "reading to learn" by providing even more text, varied writing styles, and less familiar topics.

Whichever book is right for your reader, Blastoff! Readers are the perfect books to build confidence and encourage a love of reading that will last a lifetime!

This edition first published in 2014 by Bellwether Media, Inc.

No part of this publication may be reproduced in whole or in part without written permission of the publisher. For information regarding permission, write to Bellwether Media, Inc., Attention: Permissions Department, 5357 Penn Avenue South, Minneapolis, MN 55419.

Library of Congress Cataloging-in-Publication Data

Schuetz, Kristin.
  Washington / by Kristin Schuetz.
    pages cm. – (Blastoff! readers. Exploring the states)
  Includes bibliographical references and index.
  Summary: "Developed by literacy experts for students in grades three through seven, this book introduces young readers to the geography and culture of Washington"– Provided by publisher.
  ISBN 978-1-62617-047-6 (hardcover : alk. paper)
  1. Washington (State)–Juvenile literature. I. Title.
  F891.3.S38 2014
  979.7–dc23
                                                                        2013011049

Printed in the United States of America, North Mankato, MN.

Table of Contents

Strait of
Juan de Fuca

San Juan Islands

Puget
Sound

Seattle

Tacoma

Olympia

Mount Rainier

Pacific Ocean

Washington

Columbia River

Oregon

Washington sits in the northwestern corner of the
contiguous United States. It covers an area of 68,095
square miles (176,365 square kilometers). Idaho and the
Snake River border Washington to the east. The Columbia
River and Oregon lie to the south. Canada's westernmost
province, British Columbia, shares Washington's
northern border.

The Pacific Ocean touches western Washington. It connects to the narrow **Strait** of Juan de Fuca and then to Puget **Sound**. The San Juan Islands are located within Puget Sound. Orcas, San Juan, Shaw, and Lopez are the major islands. Smaller islands dot the waters around them. The southern end of Puget Sound touches Olympia, Washington's capital.

The first people to dwell in Washington were the Chinook, Yakama, and other **Native** Americans. European and American explorers did not arrive until the late 1700s and early 1800s. In 1805, Meriwether Lewis and William Clark traveled down the Columbia River while exploring the West. Fur traders and loggers made their way to Washington, too. The territory became the forty-second state in 1889.

Yakama Native American warrior

Washington Timeline!

1774: Juan Pérez explores the Northwest coast for Spain.

1805: American explorers Meriwether Lewis and William Clark follow the Columbia River through Washington.

1811: Fort Okanogan becomes the first American fur trading post in Washington.

1889: Washington becomes the forty-second state.

1897-1898: Seattle becomes a "Gateway to Alaska" during the Klondike Gold Rush.

1899: Mount Rainier becomes the fifth national park in the U.S.

1962: The Space Needle observation tower opens for the World's Fair in Seattle.

1980: Mount St. Helens erupts. The volcanic activity kills 57 people and causes a great amount of damage.

Lewis and Clark

Space Needle

Mount St. Helens eruption

The Land

Washington's Climate
average °F

spring
Low: 39°
High: 60°

summer
Low: 52°
High: 78°

fall
Low: 40°
High: 61°

winter
Low: 30°
High: 43°

Cascade Mountains

The Cascade Mountains divide Washington into east and west sections. The range has a chain of **volcanoes**, including Mount Rainier and Mount St. Helens. The Columbia **Plateau** spreads across most of eastern Washington. Apple orchards, wheat fields, and vineyards cover its hills and valleys.

The Olympic **Peninsula** is in the west. This landscape is known for its rugged beaches and the Olympic Mountains. A tall **canopy** of Sitka spruce and western hemlock trees covers the Hoh, a **temperate rain forest** on the peninsula. Some of its trees are 300 feet (91 meters) tall!

Hoh Rain Forest

! fun fact

More than 12 feet (3.7 meters) of rain falls in the Hoh Rain Forest each year!

Mount Rainier

Did you know?

Around 20 small earthquakes shake the base of Mount Rainier each year. Only Mount St. Helens has more earthquake activity in the northern Cascades.

Mount Rainier towers higher than any other peak in the Cascades or the entire state. It rises to 14,410 feet (4,392 meters). Ice patches and 25 major **glaciers** cover the volcanic mountain. Its three large peaks are snowcapped.

Forests cover the base of the giant mountain. In summer, wildflower meadows spring to life just above the forests. Waterfalls and lakes are also scattered around Rainier. A tiny pool of water, Lake Muriel, lies in a cave at the top of the mountain. It stays heated from Rainier's volcanic gases.

Wildlife

Much of Washington provides homes for forest animals. Roosevelt elk and black-tailed deer eat plants and moss from tree trunks. Northern spotted owls sit high above in treetops. In the Cascades, mountain goats and mountain lions climb rocky land with ease. Furry Olympic marmots love to play high in the mountain meadows.

Sea otters, seals, and harbor porpoises swim in the cool waters of the Pacific Ocean. Washington's rivers and streams welcome salmon that come to lay eggs. Orca whales can be seen feeding in the San Juan Islands. **Tide pools** hold sea stars and other mysterious creatures.

Roosevelt elk

Olympic marmot

northern spotted owl

orca whale

13

Seattle is home to many of Washington's most visited landmarks. The Space Needle pokes 605 feet (184 meters) into the sky above the city. It is an observation tower that was built for the 1962 World's Fair. Today, it still offers visitors incredible **aerial** views. The famous Pike Place Market is also located in Seattle. **Vendors** sell fresh food, flowers, and other unique items.

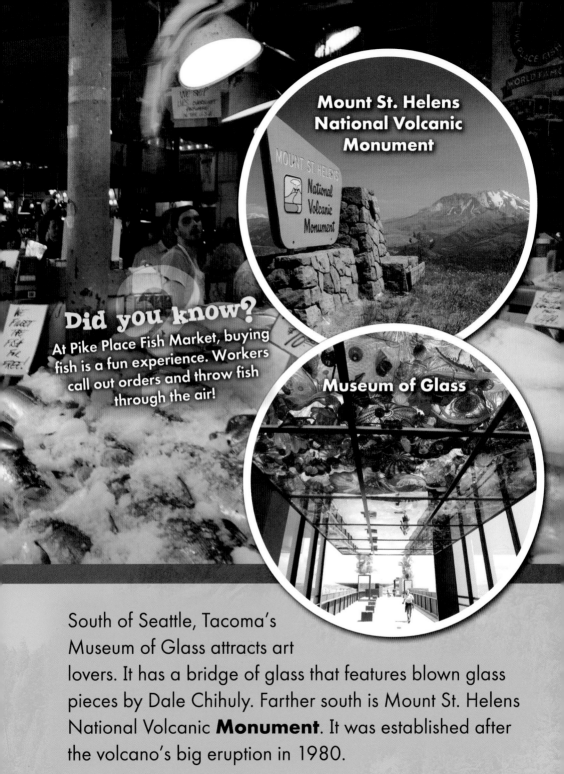

Mount St. Helens National Volcanic Monument

Did you know?
At Pike Place Fish Market, buying fish is a fun experience. Workers call out orders and throw fish through the air!

Museum of Glass

South of Seattle, Tacoma's Museum of Glass attracts art lovers. It has a bridge of glass that features blown glass pieces by Dale Chihuly. Farther south is Mount St. Helens National Volcanic **Monument**. It was established after the volcano's big eruption in 1980.

Seattle

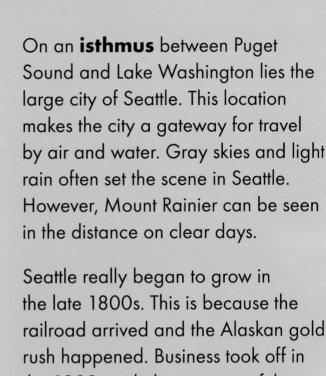

On an **isthmus** between Puget Sound and Lake Washington lies the large city of Seattle. This location makes the city a gateway for travel by air and water. Gray skies and light rain often set the scene in Seattle. However, Mount Rainier can be seen in the distance on clear days.

Seattle really began to grow in the late 1800s. This is because the railroad arrived and the Alaskan gold rush happened. Business took off in the 1900s with the creation of the Boeing aircraft company. Today the city is a center of technology and the arts. Its residents enjoy books, films, and live music.

! fun fact

Seattle has the world's two longest floating bridges. The bridges connect Seattle to cities across Lake Washington.

Many Washingtonians work in **manufacturing**. Some make airplanes for The Boeing Company. Others produce computer software at Microsoft. Workers also craft wood products from the state's timber. **Service jobs** are another common area of employment. People work in restaurants and coffee shops that serve **tourists**. They also work in schools, hospitals, and banks.

Fishers get out on the water to catch salmon, crab, and other seafood. Farmers raise beef cattle and dairy cows. At apple orchards, workers pick ripe apples by hand. More than ten billion apples are hand-picked each year in Washington!

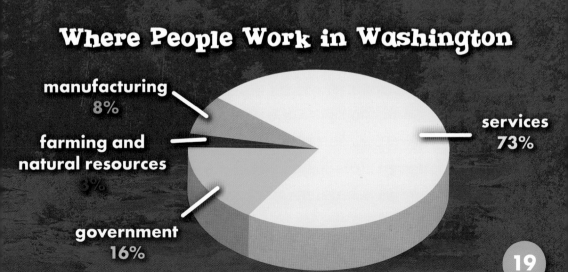

Where People Work in Washington

- manufacturing 8%
- farming and natural resources 3%
- government 16%
- services 73%

Washington's lush forests provide a natural playground for hikers and campers. Mount Rainier and other tall peaks challenge climbers. Skiers and snowboarders make their way down powdered peaks. The Ski to Sea Race takes relay teams from the snowy mountains to the waters of Bellingham Bay. Team members ski, run, bike, canoe, and kayak.

Many people in Washington enjoy water activities. Rowing, paddleboarding, and fishing are all favorites. Whale watchers take boat rides to the San Juan Islands to see orca, minke, gray, and humpback whales. They often witness whales jumping out of the water! When no whales are in sight, visitors see other sea life such as seals.

Dutch Baby

Ingredients:

- 3 eggs
- 1/2 cup flour
- 1/2 cup milk
- 1 tablespoon sugar
- 4 tablespoons butter
- Pinch of nutmeg

Topping:

- Fresh fruit
- Powdered sugar

Directions:

1. Preheat oven to 425°F.

2. Combine eggs, flour, milk, sugar, and nutmeg. Mix well.

3. Place butter in a heavy skillet or baking dish and place in the oven. Watch carefully. When the butter has melted, remove from oven and add batter to the pan. Return pan to oven and bake for 20 minutes until pancake is puffy and golden. Lower temperature to 300°F and bake for 5 more minutes.

4. Remove pancake from oven. Slice into wedges and top with fresh fruit and powdered sugar. Serve immediately.

salmon

Fresh seafood is the most common meal for many Washingtonians. Salmon, oysters, and crab are favorites. The native way to prepare salmon was to cook it on wooden planks or sticks over a fire. Some people still use this **traditional** method today. Clams often end up in a thick, creamy soup called chowder. Other ingredients include potatoes and onions.

Washingtonians fill up on juicy fruits, too. The state grows more apples, sweet cherries, and red raspberries than any other state. Sometimes fruit tops a Dutch baby. This sweet, thick pancake was first served at Manca's Café in Seattle. A cup of coffee goes great with this breakfast treat.

Washington State International Kite Festival

There are many events to celebrate in Washington. Seafair is a summer festival in the Puget Sound area. It features a torchlight parade, air show, and pirates. Every Labor Day weekend, Seattle hosts a popular festival for the arts called Bumbershoot. Visitors experience great music, comedy, films, and more.

Seafair

Sequim Lavender Festival

The city of Sequim displays its lavender to the world each summer. People tour lavender fields and buy lavender products. The Washington State International Kite Festival is an annual event along the coast. Festivalgoers watch as kite fliers make their colorful kites dance in the sky. Seafood festivals are also common. OysterFest holds the West Coast Oyster **Shucking** Championships.

Northwest Tribal Art

Washington is a state with a big arts presence. Northwest tribal art is among the most visible around the state. This form of art focuses on the natural world. Works often include creatures such as orca whales, bears, eagles, and ravens. Each animal represents different qualities.

Totem poles are common sights throughout Washington. However, this was not always the case. Washington's first totem pole was actually taken from Alaska! Artists in Washington started carving totem poles when the state became the "Gateway to Alaska." The tall posts marked Washington as a center of many different cultures.

fun fact

Northwest tribal legends say that the tricky raven gave humans the sun. He stole light and brought it to the edge of the world. Then he put it in the sky and it became the sun.

Fast Facts About Washington

Washington's Flag

Washington's state flag is green to reflect its nickname, the Evergreen State. In the center is the state seal. This has a picture of George Washington, the first President of the United States. The state is named after him.

State Flower
coast rhododendron

State Nickname:	The Evergreen State
State Motto:	*Alki*; "By and By"
Year of Statehood:	1889
Capital City:	Olympia
Other Major Cities:	Seattle, Spokane, Tacoma
Population:	6,724,540 (2010)
Area:	68,095 square miles (176,365 square kilometers); Washington is the 18th largest state.
Major Industries:	manufacturing, services, technology, farming, fishing, tourism
Natural Resources:	timber, waterpower, sand, gravel
State Government:	98 representatives; 49 senators
Federal Government:	10 representatives; 2 senators
Electoral Votes:	12

State Animal
orca whale

State Bird
willow goldfinch

Glossary

aerial—from high in the air

canopy—a thick covering of leafy branches formed by the tops of trees

contiguous—touching and connected

glaciers—massive sheets of ice that cover large areas of land

isthmus—a narrow strip of land that connects two larger pieces of land

manufacturing—the business of making goods from basic materials

monument—a protected area of land that is similar to a national park

native—originally from a specific place

peninsula—a section of land that extends out from a larger piece of land and is almost completely surrounded by water

plateau—an area of flat, raised land

province—an area within a country; a province follows all the laws of the country and makes some of its own laws.

service jobs—jobs that perform tasks for people or businesses

shucking—removing the shell of an oyster or other shellfish

sound—a long, wide extension of the ocean into land

strait—a narrow stretch of water that connects two larger bodies of water

temperate rain forest—a forest of evergreen and broadleaf trees that receives a lot of rain; temperate rain forests grow in places with mild temperatures.

tide pools—rocky pools of saltwater near the ocean

tourists—people who travel to visit another place

traditional—relating to a custom, idea, or belief handed down from one generation to the next

vendors—people who sell goods

volcanoes—holes in the earth; when a volcano erupts, hot, melted rock called lava shoots out.

To Learn More

AT THE LIBRARY
Dell, Pamela. *Welcome to Mount Rainier National Park*. Chanhassen, Minn.: Child's World, 2007.

Leon, Vicki. *A Pod of Killer Whales: The Mysterious Life of the Intelligent Orca*. Montrose, Calif.: London Town Press, 2006.

Webster, Christine. *Washington*. New York, N.Y.: Children's Press, 2009.

ON THE WEB
Learning more about Washington is as easy as 1, 2, 3.

1. Go to www.factsurfer.com.

2. Enter "Washington" into the search box.

3. Click the "Surf" button and you will see a list of related Web sites.

With factsurfer.com, finding more information is just a click away.

Index

The images in this book are reproduced through the courtesy of: tusharkoley, front cover; Lucullus Virgil McWhorter/ Internet Archives/ Wikipedia, p. 6; The Art Gallery Collection/ Alamy, p. 7 (left); (Collection)/ Prints & Photographs Division/ Library of Congress, p. 7 (middle); Exactostock/ SuperStock, p. 7 (right); tusharkoley, pp. 8-9; Steve Bower, p. 9 (small); Christopher Boswell, pp. 10-11; Tom Reichner, p. 12 (top); Mark R, p. 12 (middle); Jared Hobbs/ GlowImages, p. 12 (bottom); Thomas Kitchin & Vict/ All Canada Photos/ SuperStock, pp. 12-13; AP Photo/ Ted S. Warren file, pp. 14-15; Andre Jenny Stock Connection Worldwide/ Newscom, p. 15 (top); Zach Holmes/ Alamy, p. 15 (bottom); Lonnie Gorsline, pp. 16-17; PhilAugustavo, p. 17 (small); Monty Rakusen Cultura/ Newscom, p. 18; CandyBox Images, p. 19; NaturePL/ SuperStock, pp. 20-21; Ipatov, p. 21 (top); Candice Cusack, p. 21 (bottom); Lulu Durand, p. 22; Brent Hofacker, p. 23; Mazdaguy03, p. 23 (small); Danita Delimont/ Alamy, pp. 24-25; Paul Fell, p. 25 (top); Danita Delimont/ Getty Images, p. 25 (bottom); Andrea Izzotti, p. 26; Emily Riddell/ AgeFotoStock, pp. 26-27; Pakmor, p. 28 (top); Sascha Preussner, p. 28 (bottom); Al Mueller, p. 28 (left); Mike Liu, p. 28 (right).